NOTTINGHAM
THEN & NOW

IN COLOUR

DOUGLAS WHITWORTH

The
History
Press

The demolition of the rock houses in Sneinton Hermitage in 1897.

First published in 2011
This edition printed 2015

The History Press
The Mill, Brimscombe Port
Stroud, Gloucestershire, GL5 2QG
www.thehistorypress.co.uk

British Library Cataloguing in Publication Data.
A catalogue record for this book is available from the British Library.

ISBN 978 0 7509 6374 9

Typesetting and origination by The History Press
Printed in China.

CONTENTS

ACKNOWLEDGEMENTS

I wish to thank Martin Sentance for again allowing me the use of Frank Stevenson's photographs. I am also grateful to the following for the loan of prints: Alliance Boots, Geoff Blore, Judith Buist, the City of Nottingham Local Studies Library, Clive Hardy, John Lock, John Middleton and William Palmer. The colour photographs are my own work.

I am also indebted to Dorothy Ritchie and the staff of the Local Studies Library for their unfailing kindness and assistance. My thanks are also due to the following for their help in the production of this book: Darren Cox, Ralph Gee, Trevor Howes, Philip Johnson, Don Press, Fay Smith and Alan Trease.

Finally, I should like to express my gratitude to my wife Margaret, whose help and advice have been so greatly appreciated.

ABOUT THE AUTHOR

Douglas Whitworth has been an amateur photographer since the end of the Second World War, and since then he has photographed Nottingham, London and Paris and has been compiling books of photographs for the last twenty-five years. Douglas's other books include *A Century of Nottingham, Nottingham in the 1960s & 70s* and *London: Life in the Post-War Years,* published by The History Press.

INTRODUCTION

A book of comparison photographs is obviously only of interest if there is a significant difference between the old image and the new one. This selection of pictures is a personal choice of Nottingham's buildings and scenes which have changed during the twentieth century.

Among these illustrations are numerous examples of missed opportunities by the city council and by local companies. Drury Hill, which was demolished in 1969, could have been incorporated into the scheme to build the Broad Marsh Shopping Centre. The lamented Black Boy Hotel would still be enhancing Long Row today if there had been sufficient consideration of the issues of conservation in the 1960s.

The construction of the Victoria Railway Station in the late 1890s caused the demolition of a whole neighbourhood of old houses, over twenty public houses and the Nottingham Union Workhouse. The station, which remained for fewer than seventy years, is remembered with affection by many Nottingham people. Its clock tower, which was saved from destruction, is now almost dwarfed by the nearby Victoria Centre flats.

The First World War brought a halt to further changes in the city, but in the 1920s Friar Lane was widened, with the consequent loss of Dorothy Vernon's dwelling – a medieval house built on the site of a Carmelite friary. Towards the end of the 1920s the Great Market Place was the scene of a great transformation when the Exchange was demolished, along with the warren of shops, stalls and public houses at the rear.

The dazzlingly white Council House which replaced the Exchange came as a great shock to the citizens of Nottingham, and it was some time before the new town hall became fully accepted. The loss of the covered market and the removal of the Goose Fair from the Market Place following the construction of the Processional Way caused a public outcry – but to no avail.

Fortunately, Nottingham was not too severely damaged by enemy raids in the Second World War and the city council felt no urgency to plan and rebuild. When rebuilding in the city centre began again in the 1950s the first major project was the construction of Maid Marian Way from Canal Street to Chapel Bar. This was the first part of a proposed inner ring road which cut a swathe through some of Nottingham's oldest streets and saw the demolition of the Collin's Almhouses on Friar Lane.

The land previously occupied by the Victoria Railway Station and Broad Marsh was conveniently available when new-style shopping centres were being planned in Britain.

Following protests at the despoiling of the city centre in the 1950s and 1960s the city council took heed of public opinion and began a policy of conservation rather than wholesale destruction.

This selection of photographs gives the reader an opportunity to see some of the changes which have occurred in Nottingham in the twentieth century – and to make their own judgement on them.

LOWER PARLIAMENT STREET

BASS & WILFORD'S chemist shop on Lower Parliament Street in the 1880s (left), with advertisements for patent medicines covering the façade and the hanging lamp. This was the shop to which William Howitt, the Quaker and writer, brought his bride Mary in 1823. The Howitts became well-known poets and entertained William and Dorothy Wordsworth and Robert and Elizabeth Browning, among other writers, at their later home in the Great Market Place. On the left is the Original Dog and Partridge public house, so-named to distinguish it from the Old Dog and Partridge on the opposite side of Parliament Street. These premises were pulled down in 1896 to be replaced by an enlarged Original Dog and Partridge, itself demolished in 1970 to be replaced by a Boots store.

THE FAÇADE OF the Victoria Shopping Centre is an example of the 1970s style of architecture: bland concrete and glass. Replacing the Original Dog and Partridge, as well as several small shops and the Milton's Head Hotel, the huge centre is scheduled to be extended even further north.

THE
TRADESMEN'S
MART

THIS BUILDING (RIGHT), known as the Tradesmen's Mart, was one of the more distinctive features of Lower Parliament Street in the 1890s. The style of architecture was unique in Nottingham, with balconied dwellings above the shops and railed areas with steps leading down to the basements. The businesses here included a printer, an umbrella-maker, a portmanteau-maker, a tinsmith, and a boot and shoemaker. The building was demolished in 1897 and Lombard House was built here in 1901 for use by a fruit and potato merchant. In 1910, R. Cripps & Company established their main car showroom here and were to remain for the following sixty years.

TODAY THE BUILDING is occupied by Argos as a catalogue warehouse – a modern trading outlet undreamt of by the occupiers of the old Tradesmen's Mart.

THE VICTORIA RAILWAY STATION

THE VICTORIA RAILWAY Station in 1953 (left), when travel to all parts of the country by rail was still possible. The station remained for another fourteen years before it was closed under the Beeching axe. The trolleybus in the foreground is a Notts. & Derbys. Traction Co. vehicle on the Ripley to Nottingham service, one of the longest routes in the country. This was the year these trolleybuses ceased operation.

FOLLOWING THE DEMOLITION of the Victoria Railway Station's tracks, platforms and booking hall in 1967, the Victoria Shopping Centre and flats were built, leaving the clock tower as a monument to a past age. Since the decline of the Broad Marsh Shopping Centre, the Victoria Centre has become the busiest shopping area in Nottingham, drawing trade away from the city centre.

11

THE MECHANICS CINEMA

THE MECHANICS CINEMA in 1950 (below). This cinema, as with the nearby Lounge Cinema, was converted from a public hall and was not ideal for showing films. The hall was built in 1869 to replace an earlier building which had been destroyed by fire. Many famous personalities appeared here, including Captain R.F. Scott, Sir Ernest Shackleton, Oscar Wilde and Sir Arthur Conan Doyle. The hall was also the venue for events ranging from recitals and religious meetings to displays of weightlifting and demonstrations of the phonograph. In 1916 the hall became a cinema – the seats

along each side of the balcony giving only restricted views. The films being shown here at the time of the photograph were *The Rugged O'Riordans* with John O'Malley and *Buccaneer's Girl* starring Yvonne de Carlo. This was the heyday of cinema-going, and programmes then consisted of two feature films and a newsreel.

FOLLOWING THE CLOSURE of the Mechanics Cinema in 1964, Birkbeck House, named after the founder of the Mechanics Institutes, was built here. In 2008, this building was replaced by a monolithic structure, part of the Trinity Square development.

SHAKESPEARE STREET

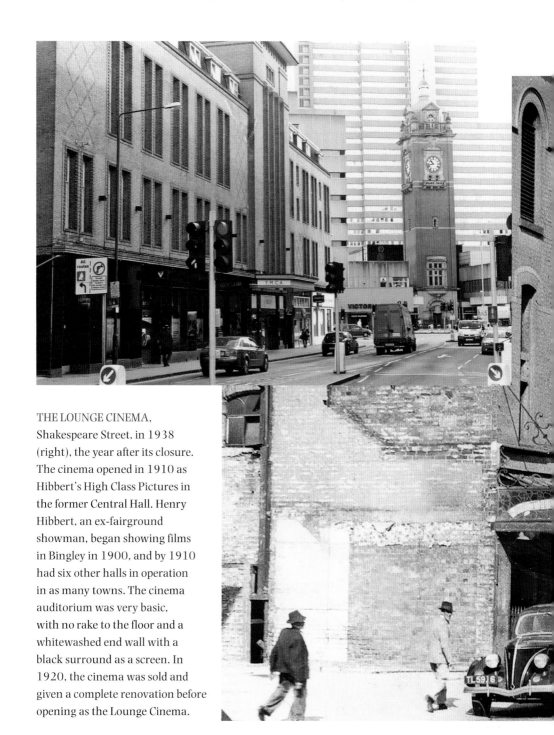

THE LOUNGE CINEMA, Shakespeare Street, in 1938 (right), the year after its closure. The cinema opened in 1910 as Hibbert's High Class Pictures in the former Central Hall. Henry Hibbert, an ex-fairground showman, began showing films in Bingley in 1900, and by 1910 had six other halls in operation in as many towns. The cinema auditorium was very basic, with no rake to the floor and a whitewashed end wall with a black surround as a screen. In 1920, the cinema was sold and given a complete renovation before opening as the Lounge Cinema.

AFTER THE DEMOLITION of the old properties, the Young Men's Christian Association premises were built on the site. When completed in 1941, the building included a chapel, concert hall, gymnasium and forty bedrooms, which were used during the war by the armed forces. Today the YMCA provides accommodation for the homeless, besides retaining the chapel, and it also has a rehabilitation centre and a health and fitness centre.

THE *GUARDIAN* OFFICE

THE *GUARDIAN* OFFICE decorated for the coronation of Queen Elizabeth II in 1953 (left).
Thomas Forman took over the publication of the *Nottinghamshire Guardian* in 1849 when it was
then printed on Long Row. When he wished to expand his business, Thomas Forman bought
land at the junction of South Sherwood Street and North Street in 1870 and built new premises
at a cost of £10,000.

The *Nottingham Evening Post* began publication in 1878 and now remains the only daily paper printed by the Nottingham Post Group. Over the years other titles have come and gone, including the *Post Buff,* which was published in the summer months at the close of each day's play of cricket. Older readers may remember 'Knocker Post', who would call at homes and give ten shillings to anyone who could produce a current copy of the *Evening Post*. Publication of the *Evening Post* ceased here in 1998. The editorial departments are now in City Gate, Tollhouse Hill, with the newspaper being printed in Birmingham.

THE CORNERHOUSE AT the junction of South Sherwood Street and Forman Street in 2003.
This leisure and entertainment centre opened in 2001 on the site of the *Nottingham Evening
Post* offices. The nearby Theatre Square was already the heart of Nottingham's nightlife when
this concrete and glass building opened. The complex, with fourteen cinema screens, has now
replaced the ABC and the Odeon – the last two city centre cinemas. The Cornerhouse also
contains over twenty bars and cafés as well as a fitness centre and shops. At night the building
glows with vivid lights, drawing both young and not-so-young to its many attractions.

THE EMPIRE PALACE
OF VARIETIES

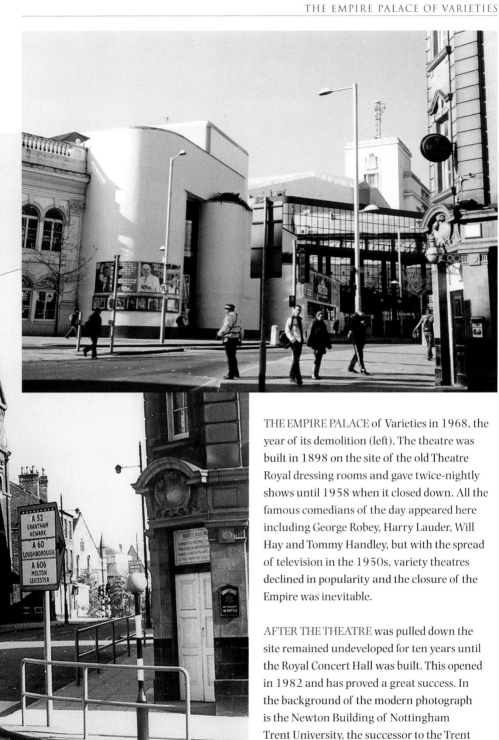

THE EMPIRE PALACE of Varieties in 1968, the year of its demolition (left). The theatre was built in 1898 on the site of the old Theatre Royal dressing rooms and gave twice-nightly shows until 1958 when it closed down. All the famous comedians of the day appeared here including George Robey, Harry Lauder, Will Hay and Tommy Handley, but with the spread of television in the 1950s, variety theatres declined in popularity and the closure of the Empire was inevitable.

AFTER THE THEATRE was pulled down the site remained undeveloped for ten years until the Royal Concert Hall was built. This opened in 1982 and has proved a great success. In the background of the modern photograph is the Newton Building of Nottingham Trent University, the successor to the Trent Polytechnic. To the right is the recently renamed Turf Tavern public house.

19

THEATRE SQUARE

THEATRE SQUARE WITH tram
No. 67 bound for Radford in 1934
(right) – the last year of use on this
route. Trams were finally replaced
by trolleybuses in 1936, a form of
transport which was superseded by
motorbuses in 1966. The motorcyclist
attempting to overtake the tram
perhaps imagines he is on a speedway
track. Above Parker's tobacconist
shop is the once familiar Player's
Navy Cut sign.

NOTTINGHAM'S TRAMS ARE now
running again and a new generation

of citizens are becoming accustomed to this old form of transport in an updated version. These vehicles, which glide speedily along the city streets, gave Nottingham a modern image at the beginning of a new century. The Theatre Royal, purchased by the city council in 1969, was completely restored without losing any of its character.

CHAPEL BAR

CHAPEL BAR IN 1961 (left). With the planned extension of Maid Marian Way to Chapel Bar, these buildings were already scheduled for demolition. The corner property occupied by Hickling's was, in the early eighteenth century, the home of the mayor, Thomas Hawksley. On the extreme left is the Odd Hour Cinema, also awaiting demolition. This cinema was opened in 1914 as the Parliament Street Picture House and after two changes of name became the News Theatre in 1935.

THE AREA HAS been redeveloped with offices, shops and bars. An underpass which was mistakenly constructed at this junction has now been demolished.

THE CANNON FILM CENTRE

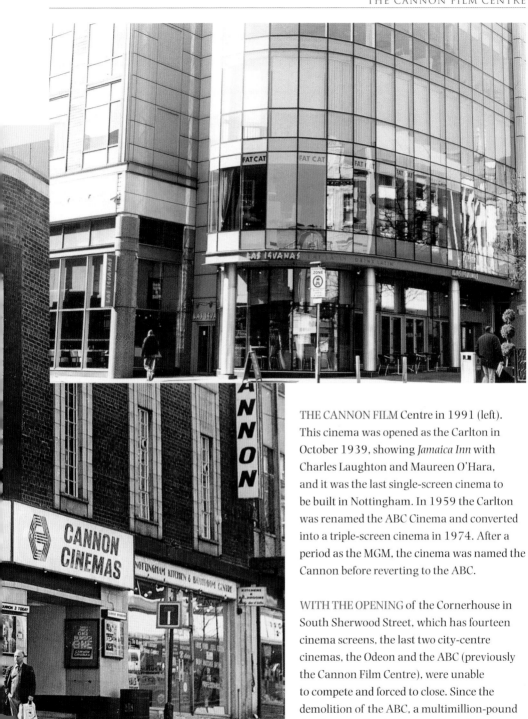

THE CANNON FILM Centre in 1991 (left). This cinema was opened as the Carlton in October 1939, showing *Jamaica Inn* with Charles Laughton and Maureen O'Hara, and it was the last single-screen cinema to be built in Nottingham. In 1959 the Carlton was renamed the ABC Cinema and converted into a triple-screen cinema in 1974. After a period as the MGM, the cinema was named the Cannon before reverting to the ABC.

WITH THE OPENING of the Cornerhouse in South Sherwood Street, which has fourteen cinema screens, the last two city-centre cinemas, the Odeon and the ABC (previously the Cannon Film Centre), were unable to compete and forced to close. Since the demolition of the ABC, a multimillion-pound development has been erected on the site. Named Chapel Quarter, the building consists of a hotel, bars, restaurants and offices.

LONG ROW

THE GREAT MARKET Place, around 1900, before electric trams had made their appearance on the streets of Nottingham. In the foreground is a rank of hansom cabs and a wagon, which was still the general-purpose carrier. To the right, Brigida Capocci is standing behind her ice cream stall – she and her compatriot Mrs Solari were well-known ice cream vendors for many years. On the left

is the entrance to the Talbot, a Victorian drinking palace with extravagant decorations and statuary. Griffin and Spalding's department store, in the centre, was founded in 1846 and in 1886 moved into this new building at the corner of Market Street. In the background is the Exchange and the town hall, designed in 1724 by the mayor, Marmaduke Pennel and largely rebuilt in 1815. Besides the council chamber and mayor's apartments, the Exchange contained numerous shops, public houses and butcher's stalls – the Shambles.

TODAY ONLY THE Talbot, now known as Yates's, remains of these buildings. One of the city's most famous haunts, this hostelry has a history extending over 400 years. Originally a Tudor inn, the building was demolished in 1874 by Edward Cox who created the most ornate gin palace in the Midlands. Griffin & Spalding's department store was rebuilt in Portland stone in the 1920s – later becoming Debenhams. The Exchange was superseded in 1929 by the new Council House – which received mixed reviews; some citizens considered the Council House too grandiose, while others believed it added stature to Nottingham. The latter view has generally prevailed.

THE BLACK BOY HOTEL

THE BLACK BOY Hotel on Long Row, 1952 (right). This was the heyday of the hotel, when Commonwealth cricket teams stayed here, although the deep tones of Little John in the nearby Council House dome were apparently not to their liking! The hotel was built in 1887 by Watson Fothergill on the site of an earlier inn and enlarged in 1897. The interior was ornate, and the public rooms included several bars and restaurants as well as a smoking room and a ladies' room. When the hotel closed in 1969 Nottingham lost one of its most famous and attractive buildings. This stretch of Long Row also possessed many well-known retailers including several shoe shops such as Barratts, Stead & Simpson, Manfield & Sons and Craddocks. Other shops were Sodens who claimed to be court furriers, Stanley Dennis the hairdresser, Sands the milliner and Skinner & Rook the high-class provisioner and wine merchant.

A FACELESS BRANCH of Littlewoods was built to replace the Black Boy Hotel, a structure which completely spoils this parade. The only concession to tradition is the colonnade on Long Row.

WATSON FOTHERGILL'S NOTTINGHAM AND NOTTS. BANK

A REAR VIEW of the Natwest Bank on Thurland Street in 1988 (left). This sight was possible for a time when the building at the corner of Clumber Street and Pelham Street was demolished. The building was designed by Watson Fothergill in 1882 for the Nottingham & Notts. Bank and has a façade resplendent with architectural detail. The round banking hall is notable for its stained glass windows and fine sculptures. The tall tower in the background with its four turrets serves a dual purpose, being decorative and also containing the bank's ventilation system.

THIS CORNER OF Clumber Street and Pelham Street is now occupied by a modern building housing a branch of Santander. After more than a century the Watson Fothergill building is no longer a bank but a retail outlet.

HIGH STREET

HIGH STREET IN 1929 (right), as busy then as it is now. On the right is Boots the Chemist and at the corner of Long Row and Clumber Street is Skinner & Rook the grocery and wine merchant. The latter shop was well known for its freshly ground coffee, hampers of food and fine wines. The business was started by Mr Skinner in 1844 and joined by Mr Rook in 1860. The shop closed in 1955 when Skinner & Rook moved to Maypole Yard and this building was demolished. The first car on the right is a Morris Minor followed by a Bullnosed Morris.

THE JUNCTION OF Long Row and Clumber Street now has a ubiquitous office block with branches of national shops on the ground floor. The splendid art nouveau building of 1903 on the right was vacated by Boots in 1972 and is now occupied by Zara, a fashion business. This street has been pedestrianised and is on the route between Nottingham's two shopping centres. Consequently it is always crowded with people.

THE FLYING HORSE HOTEL

THE FLYING HORSE Hotel, The Poultry, in 1900 (left). The hotel bears the date 1483 and stands upon the site of the house which the Plumptre family erected when they came to Nottingham in the thirteenth century. Although much restored, it still retained the appearance of an Elizabethan coaching inn and in the past was known as the Travellers Inn. On the right is J. & A. Kirk's Midland Bonnet Emporium, whose windows are filled from top to bottom with articles for sale.

TODAY THIS STRETCH of The Poultry bears only a slight resemblance to the early years of the twentieth century. The Flying Horse is now the FH Mall, with a mock-Tudor façade which is a copy of the Rose & Crown at Saffron Walden. Since the reintroduction of trams to the city, modern vehicles regularly glide past here.

BRIDLESMITH GATE

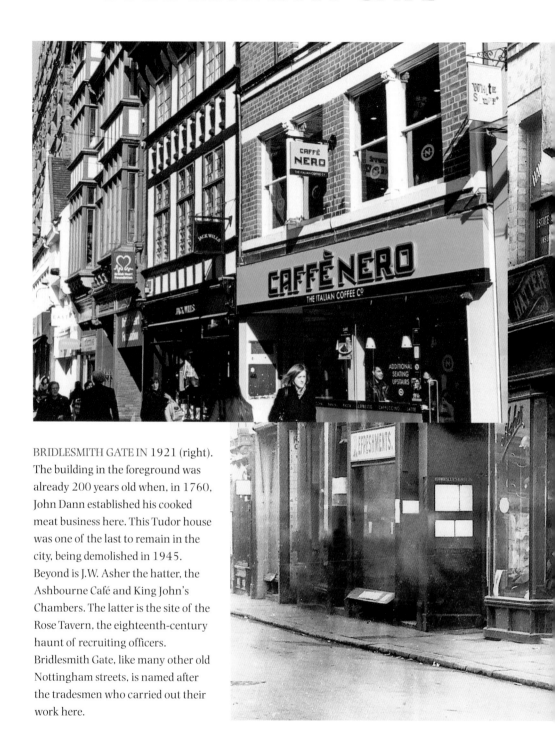

BRIDLESMITH GATE IN 1921 (right). The building in the foreground was already 200 years old when, in 1760, John Dann established his cooked meat business here. This Tudor house was one of the last to remain in the city, being demolished in 1945. Beyond is J.W. Asher the hatter, the Ashbourne Café and King John's Chambers. The latter is the site of the Rose Tavern, the eighteenth-century haunt of recruiting officers. Bridlesmith Gate, like many other old Nottingham streets, is named after the tradesmen who carried out their work here.

NEW BUILDINGS HAVE replaced the first two old structures on Bridlesmith Gate – the timber-framed building has been preserved, although passed almost unnoticed by the stream of pedestrians who frequent this precinct.

ST PETER'S GATE

ST PETER'S GATE, *c*.1895 (left). This was the terminus for horse-trams, which ran to London Road and Trent Bridge. The services were run by the Nottingham & District Tramway Co., which started in 1878 and was superseded in 1897 by the Nottingham Corporation. On the left is Alexander's, advertised as the Great Clothier, and across Exchange Walk is Marriott Bros, ironmongers, who were to remain for another half century. Beyond is the Eight Bells public house, which was used for a scene in the film *Saturday Night and Sunday Morning* shortly after its closure in 1959.

ST PETER'S GATE is no longer a through road for vehicles, and shoppers crossing from Exchange Walk to the multiple stores beyond are unhindered by traffic. The Eight Bells and the adjoining building have been replaced by offices and shops – the street has thereby lost a great deal of character.

WHEELER GATE

WHEELER GATE, c.1928 (right). This
is a street of mainly Victorian buildings
with many businesses unknown to the
younger citizens of Nottingham. On the
corner of Hounds Gate is Vernon Heaton,
advertising London suitings, and next door
is Alexandres, then a well-known outfitter.
Beyond are two popular cafés, the Savoy
and Morley's, and further up Wheeler Gate
is the Oriental Café – none of which have
survived. On the opposite side of the street
is the Horse & Groom, which dates from
the seventeenth century, and beyond is the
Canadian Fur Co. In the right foreground
a traffic policeman is standing on his box,
with only light traffic to direct.

ONCE THE ROAD from the south to the
city centre, this is now a one-way street
northwards. In the recent photograph,

tall office blocks fill the sky, but trees have been planted to soften their impact. Many of the city centre's roads have now been pedestrianised, but Wheeler Gate has become the site of Nottingham's main taxi rank.

DOROTHY VERNON'S HOUSE

DOROTHY VERNON'S HOUSE, Priory Courtyard off Friar Lane, in 1921 (left). This was the house in which John Manners and Dorothy Vernon lived after their elopement from Haddon Hall in 1572. The property was built on the site of a ruined Carmelite Friary, which had existed for 300 years until the Dissolution of the Monasteries in 1539. When the widening of Friar Lane began in 1922, Dorothy Vernon's house was threatened with demolition and, despite public protests, the historic building was needlessly pulled down in 1927.

TOBY'S DEPARTMENT STORE, built in 1930 on the site of Dorothy Vernon's house, prospered for many years, but after a takeover in 1982 the shop finally closed a year later. Since then the property has had a variety of uses from an indoor market to its present function as the Approach, a bar and restaurant.

SPANIEL ROW

THE JUNCTION OF Friar Lane and Spaniel Row in 1922 (left). The house on the corner was once owned by Sheriff Reckless who, in 1649, was converted by George Fox, the founder of the Society of Friends. The Quaker was given shelter here after his imprisonment for disturbing a service in St Mary's church. Parked outside the house is a Rover 8 motorcar with its spare wheel and battery on the running board.

DURING THE ROAD widening scheme of the 1920s a number of historical buildings were demolished including the buildings on Spaniel Row. The replacements are anonymous office blocks which passers-by rarely notice. The only reminder of the history of the area is the street name Spaniel Row, which, like the nearby Hounds Gate, refers to the spaniels kept here by monarchs during the Middle Ages.

45

THE ROYAL CHILDREN

THE SEVENTEENTH-CENTURY Royal Children inn at the corner of Castle Gate and St Nicholas Street in 1924 (right). The story of the children of Princess Anne, daughter of James II, lodging here in 1688 is a myth. The princess fled to Nottingham Castle for safety during the Glorious Revolution but at that time had no living offspring. The whalebone hanging above the entrance is genuine and a relic of the days when whale oil first supplanted candles for lighting. Regrettably, the old inn was demolished in 1933.

THE MOCK-TUDOR replacement for the Jacobean Royal Children (above). The shoulder blade of the whale, after hanging outside the inn for centuries, is now kept in a glass case inside the building.

CASTLE GATE

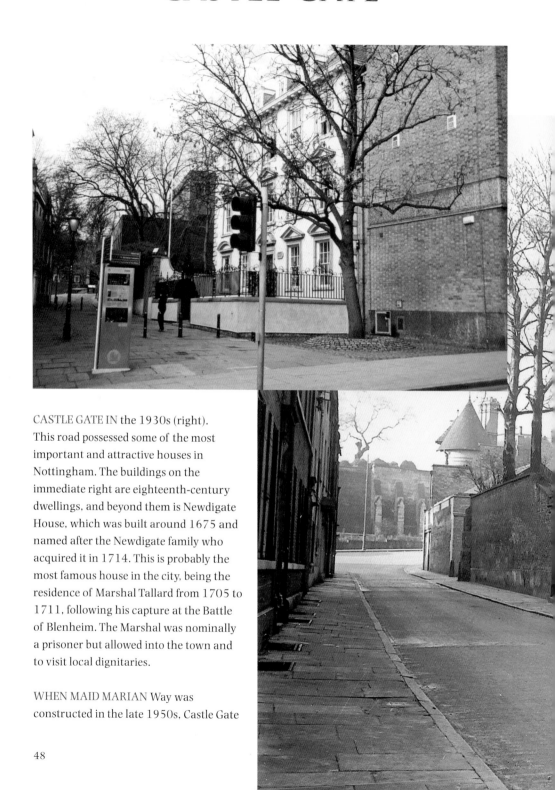

CASTLE GATE IN the 1930s (right). This road possessed some of the most important and attractive houses in Nottingham. The buildings on the immediate right are eighteenth-century dwellings, and beyond them is Newdigate House, which was built around 1675 and named after the Newdigate family who acquired it in 1714. This is probably the most famous house in the city, being the residence of Marshal Tallard from 1705 to 1711, following his capture at the Battle of Blenheim. The Marshal was nominally a prisoner but allowed into the town and to visit local dignitaries.

WHEN MAID MARIAN Way was constructed in the late 1950s, Castle Gate was bisected with the loss of the first two houses on the right. Fortunately, Newdigate House was spared but there is now a stark contrast between it and the adjoining modern office block. By the 1960s Newdigate House was in a neglected state and the city council planned to convert it into a museum, but financial restrictions prevented this. The house was then acquired by the United Services Club as their new home and now the ground floor has been opened as the World Service Restaurant.

CASTLE ROAD

CASTLE ROAD IN 1949 (left).
During the following decade, in the
indiscriminate clearance of this area,
many fine buildings were demolished.
Walnut Tree Lane, leading downhill
on the left, is a picturesque street
with a number of old and interesting
buildings. Further down Castle Road,
Jessamine Cottages – an attractive row
of houses – was pulled down in 1956
to make way for the People's College
of Further Education.

SEVERNS, A FIFTEENTH-CENTURY
merchant's house on Middle
Pavement, in danger of demolition,
was saved and re-erected here in
1970. Opened as the Lace Centre,
it was an attraction to tourists, but
unfortunately it has now closed.
Castle Road has been pedestrianised,
greatly improving the character of
the area.

THE CASTLE GATEHOUSE

THE ENTRANCE TO Nottingham Castle in 1949. The gatehouse contains the remaining fragments of the ancient castle, but these were mostly hidden when it was restored in 1908. The grounds of the

castle have always been popular with citizens and visitors, being only a short walk from the Old Market Square. The skyline was then dominated by the Classical style Council House.

THE NEW CITY House on Maid Marian Way and the Pearl Assurance building on Friar Lane now block most of the view towards the Old Market Square, and only the Nottingham Wheel is just visible – a feature which has dominated the Old Market Square in recent winters. The construction of Maid Marian Way created a barrier between the city centre and the castle, and little thought was given to the design and height of the buildings along the road and the impact they would have on the environment.

BROAD MARSH

BROAD MARSH FROM the castle walls in 1968 (left). The demolition of the shops on Carrington Street was about to begin in preparation for the building of the Broad Marsh Shopping Centre. On the left is St Nicholas' church, which was built around 1680 after the earlier church was pulled down on the orders of Colonel Hutchinson during the Civil War. In the distance, appearing almost joined, are the High Pavement Unitarian Chapel and St Mary's church.

TODAY THE VIEW is spoilt by the unsightly roof of the Castle College and the ugly Broad Marsh Centre. Both of these buildings are scheduled for redevelopment which is well overdue. The churchyard of St Nicholas is a small oasis in the middle of the modern architecture.

THE MEADOWS

THE MEADOWS VIEWED from the castle in 1949. The near distance is filled with factories and warehouses and beyond are the terrace houses built in the late nineteenth century. In the left foreground is Viyella House, designed by Frank Broadhead for William Hollins & Co. in the

early 1930s. The building was used as a factory and an office for the company's spinning and weaving business until 1961 when they moved their operations to London.

VIYELLA HOUSE, IN the left foreground above, has been renovated by the James McArtney Partnership and is now a set of offices – renamed New Castle House. The land adjoining the Nottingham Canal has been revitalised, with old warehouses restored and distinctive new buildings created. Most of the old properties in the Meadows beyond were cleared in the 1970s to be replaced with characterless homes.

THE CASTLE FROM THE MIDLAND RAILWAY

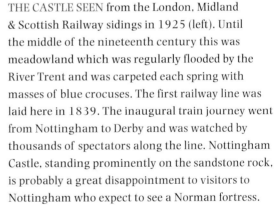

THE CASTLE SEEN from the London, Midland & Scottish Railway sidings in 1925 (left). Until the middle of the nineteenth century this was meadowland which was regularly flooded by the River Trent and was carpeted each spring with masses of blue crocuses. The first railway line was laid here in 1839. The inaugural train journey went from Nottingham to Derby and was watched by thousands of spectators along the line. Nottingham Castle, standing prominently on the sandstone rock, is probably a great disappointment to visitors to Nottingham who expect to see a Norman fortress.

THE MODERN ARCHITECTURE of the Inland Revenue building is in striking contrast to the Italianate mansion in the background. The complex was opened in 1995 and comprises seven buildings with pedestrianised streets. The amenities building, which has the appearance of a huge marquée, contains a restaurant, bar, crèche and sporting facilities.

59

NOTTINGHAM CASTLE
AND ITS ENVIRONS

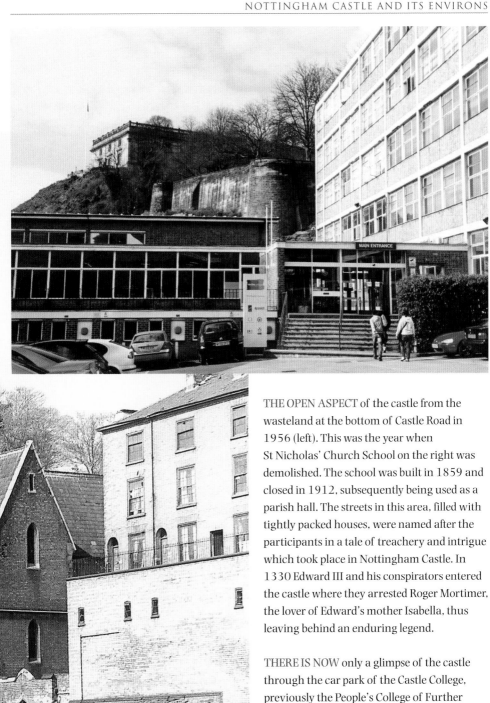

THE OPEN ASPECT of the castle from the wasteland at the bottom of Castle Road in 1956 (left). This was the year when St Nicholas' Church School on the right was demolished. The school was built in 1859 and closed in 1912, subsequently being used as a parish hall. The streets in this area, filled with tightly packed houses, were named after the participants in a tale of treachery and intrigue which took place in Nottingham Castle. In 1330 Edward III and his conspirators entered the castle where they arrested Roger Mortimer, the lover of Edward's mother Isabella, thus leaving behind an enduring legend.

THERE IS NOW only a glimpse of the castle through the car park of the Castle College, previously the People's College of Further Education. This college has a long history of higher education since it was opened on The Ropewalk in 1847 and deserves better accommodation.

61

CANAL STREET

CANAL STREET IN 1988 (left). The Narrow Boat public house in the centre was in the last few years of its life, closing down in 1996. This inn is a reminder of the heyday of the country's canals. In the background is the British Waterways building, originally the Trent Navigation warehouse, awaiting a new function.

THE WHOLE AREA has now been regenerated with old warehouses converted into a series of bars and cafés. The Bar Risa and Jongleurs Comedy Club now occupy part of the British Waterways building along with the Fitness First Health Club. The *Nottingham Evening Post* moved in 1998 from their old Forman Street building into the new offices on the right, but have since moved to City Gate, Tollhouse Hill.

THE NOTTINGHAM CANAL

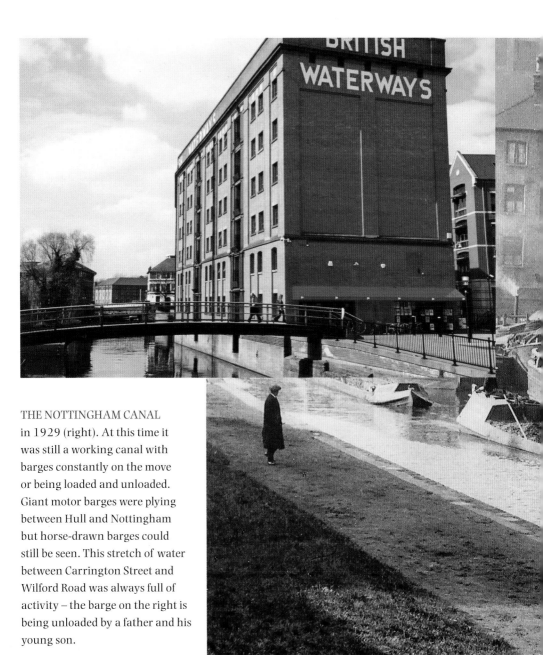

THE NOTTINGHAM CANAL in 1929 (right). At this time it was still a working canal with barges constantly on the move or being loaded and unloaded. Giant motor barges were plying between Hull and Nottingham but horse-drawn barges could still be seen. This stretch of water between Carrington Street and Wilford Road was always full of activity – the barge on the right is being unloaded by a father and his young son.

THE MODERN PICTURE shows a much more peaceful scene with only the occaisional pleasure boat in sight, although dredgers are occasionally seen. The far side of the canal has been transformed with old warehouses converted into bars and restaurants.

LISTER GATE IN 1950 (below left). This was an area with some of the largest cash-trade shops in the city. On the left are the art deco buildings of F.W. Woolworth & Co. and British Home Stores with Marks & Spencer in the distance. The Walter Fountain is on the extreme left and due for demolition. The fountain was built in 1866 by John Walter MP in memory of his father, also John Walter MP, the proprietor of *The Times*. Beyond the fountain is the Sawyers Arms, an eighteenth-century inn which was also shortly to be pulled down.

WITH THE PLANTING of the trees in this precinct the view towards the Council House has been blocked. The small ornamental fountain which was placed at the entrance to the Broad Marsh Shopping Centre as a reminder of the original edifice has now been removed.

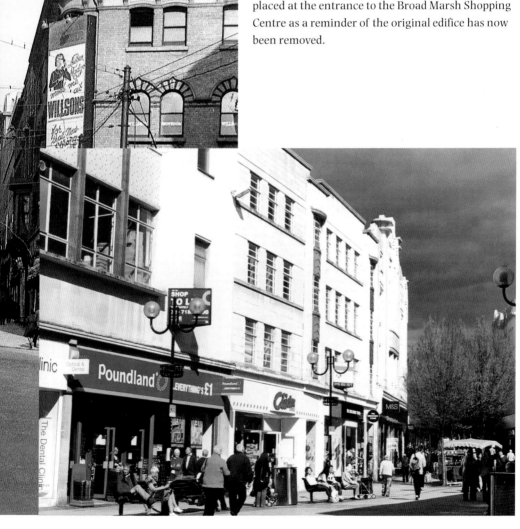

SEVERNS

SEVERNS ON MIDDLE Pavement in 1964 (left). This famous establishment was founded by John and James Severn in 1735 when they began a wine importing business here. This building, which was originally a merchant's house, is one of the oldest domestic properties in Nottingham. During the nineteenth century, Severns extended into the adjoining building when their Gentleman's Eating and Dining House had a high reputation. In 1956 the fifteenth-century building was restored but the property was not to remain here much longer as it was dismantled in 1969 and moved to Castle Road.

A NONDESCRIPT BUILDING now stands on the site of Severns, with a wine and spirit business on the ground floor. This is itself to be demolished when the Middle Pavement entrance to the Broad Marsh Centre is redeveloped.

DRURY HILL

DRURY HILL IN 1964 (right). This street was originally called Vault Lane after the huge rock cellars beneath the houses at its junction with Low Pavement. Around 1620 the street was renamed Drury Hill after Alderman Drury who then occupied Vault Hall. In the Middle Ages this street, although narrow, was an easier climb than Hollow Stone, and until the seventeenth century this was the principal entry into the town from the south. Despite protests, the buildings in this street were demolished in the late 1960s and the thoroughfare was submerged within the Broad Marsh Shopping Centre.

THIS ENTRANCE FROM Middle Pavement to the shopping centre, known as Drury Walk, leads to an escalator at the foot of which a series of caves have been opened as a tourist attraction. It is to be hoped that when the planned redevelopment of this entrance takes place, it will be more appropriate to the area.

LONG STAIRS

LONG STAIRS IN 1913 (right). This was one of the ancient routes from High Pavement down to Narrow Marsh. Halfway down the steps on the left is one of the fig trees that grew from the cliff face and which, despite the conditions, managed each year to leaf and fruit. Behind the wall on the left is Malin Hill, a path that leads down to Plumptre Square. In the distance is St Patrick's church, which opened in 1880 and was a place of worship for 100 years, closing in 1979. When the slum property was cleared from Narrow Marsh in the 1930s, Long Stairs were closed as the steps were considered too dangerous.

TODAY, ONLY AN iron gate and a few broken steps remain as a reminder of this old stairway. A fig tree still grows from the rock face, a reminder of the gardens of the great houses that once crowned this hill.

MALIN HILL

MALIN HILL CAN be seen in the photograph on the right in 1988. This bridle path from the old town, surrounding St Mary's church down to the Meadows, is probably the oldest route out of Nottingham to the south. The hill is named after George Malin who lived here at the beginning of the fourteenth century. In 1525 Sir Thomas Willoughby founded and endowed a bede house here for five poor widows.

THE RIGHT OF way down the hill has been preserved, although all the old buildings have been replaced. The Victorian Town Arms public house on the left, which suffered a serious fire in the 1980s, has also been demolished, revealing two levels of caves beneath the building.

LEEN SIDE

LEEN SIDE, LATER renamed Canal Street, viewed from Malin Hill in the 1930s (left). Most of the slum dwellings were demolished by this time and new council houses built, but some old houses remain in the foreground. At the junction of London Road and Canal Street is a YMCA hostel and, to the right, the Globe Electrical Co. with three firemen's cottages adjoining it. The building surmounted by a cupola is the Leen Side police station and mortuary and next to it is the Council School for Infants.

THE POLICE STATION, with a new building to the rear, is now the night shelter of the Nottingham Help the Homeless Association. Beyond is an apartment block and Jury's Inn, a hotel replacing a Boots office block on Station Street.

SHORT STAIRS

SHORT STAIRS IN 1913 (right). This was one of several routes from the old town around St Mary's church down to the Meadows. The earliest track was Malin Hill, dating from the Middle Ages, but in the eighteenth century both these stairs and Long Stairs were built. On the right between the two flights of steps are small dwelling-houses with clothes hanging from a washing line strung across the steps.

THE OLD HOUSES and workshops on the hillside have been demolished uncovering numerous caves in which pottery, clay pipes and other artefacts were discovered. New buildings have been erected here, and the stairs have been restored – winning a civic award.

BOOTS, ISLAND STREET

BOOTS WAREHOUSES ON Island Street in 1969 (left). These buildings were originally built as factories in 1914 and in the First World War were used to manufacture a range of goods for the troops. Boots were also responsible for the bulk of saccharin production in the country – this had previously been imported from the continent. When the Boots site opened at Beeston in the late 1920s, these buildings were converted into warehouses. In 1996 they were demolished, ending over a century of the area's association with Boots.

SEVERAL NEW BUILDINGS have been built on the thirteen-acre site. The first buildings to be constructed were the BBC Centre and a hotel but the planned apartments and marina have failed to appear.

THE HIGH LEVEL RAILWAY STATION

THE LONDON ROAD High Level Railway Station in 1935 (left). The Great Northern Railway Company built this station at the same time as the Victoria Railway Station but apart from excursion and football trains it was little used. In the 1920s and 1930s, Sunday school outings to Radcliffe-on-Trent would begin here and the station would have given the thrill of a major railway terminus to the children. The railway was closed to passenger traffic in 1967 and the bridge over London Road was demolished in 1978. The warehouses belonging to Boots in the background were to remain longer, being pulled down in 1996. In the foreground is the Nottingham Canal flowing towards the River Trent.

THE HIGH LEVEL Railway Station platforms in the earlier photograph have now been demolished and the station booking hall, which for a time was converted into Hooters, a bar-restaurant, has also been demolished. The 200-ton girder bridge carrying the railway tracks over the Nottingham Canal was removed in 1996, being lifted intact by a 1,000-ton Krupps crane before being dismantled. The site is still awaiting full development.

TRENT STREET

TRENT STREET IN 1929 (right). This
street crosses the Nottingham Canal
and replaces a wooden bridge, which
was a short-cut from the centre of the
city to the Midland Railway Station.
On the right is Atkey's motor spare
parts warehouse and one of Boots'
offices. On the left is the Great Central
viaduct, nearly a mile long, consisting
of fifty-three arches and twelve bridges,
crossing Broad Marsh, the Midland
Railway Station and the Meadows.

THE VIADUCT HAS now been replaced
by a modern structure carrying the
tram tracks towards the Nottingham
Railway Station. This line from
Hucknall was the first of three modern

tramlines built in Nottingham, each of them controversial over the route chosen. In the distance is the old High Pavement Unitarian chapel, originally converted into a lace museum but now the Pitcher and Piano, a bar and restaurant.

THE BOOTS HEAD OFFICE

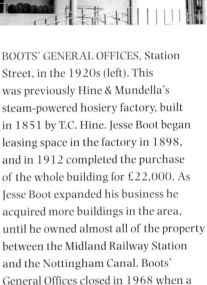

BOOTS' GENERAL OFFICES, Station Street, in the 1920s (left). This was previously Hine & Mundella's steam-powered hosiery factory, built in 1851 by T.C. Hine. Jesse Boot began leasing space in the factory in 1898, and in 1912 completed the purchase of the whole building for £22,000. As Jesse Boot expanded his business he acquired more buildings in the area, until he owned almost all of the property between the Midland Railway Station and the Nottingham Canal. Boots' General Offices closed in 1968 when a new head office opened at Beeston.

AFTER REMAINING UNDEVELOPED for thirty years, the site was first occupied by Capital One, a financial services company. The ultra-modern offices, named Loxley House, which were opened by the Prince of Wales in 2002, are now the headquarters of Nottingham City Council.

LOWER PARLIAMENT STREET

BOOTS' PRINT SERVICES (left), Lower Parliament Street, in 1988. This art deco building was constructed in 1939 for R. Cripps & Son as a garage and car showroom but was requisitioned by the Auxiliary Fire Service at the outbreak of the Second World War. In the Blitz of May 1941 this area suffered a large amount of damage and the emergency services were fully stretched. After the war, Boots used the building as a garage before converting it into offices. This building and the Nottingham Ice Stadium were demolished to make way for the National Ice Centre.

THE NATIONAL ICE Centre was opened in 2000 and has facilities for a whole range of ice sports. The complex also houses the Trent FM Arena, originally known as the Nottingham Arena, which seats 10,000 people for concerts, sporting events, ice shows and exhibitions. The Nottingham Panthers ice hockey team is based here and attracts enthusiastic spectators to the matches.

NOTINTONE PLACE

WILLIAM BOOTH, THE founder of the Salvation Army, was born in Notintone Place on
10 April 1829. The house on the left of the old photograph (right) was in a row of similar
properties and was bought by the Salvation Army in the 1930s. After the demolition of the
remainder of the terrace these houses were incorporated into an Eventide Home and Goodwill
Centre, which opened in 1971.

THE RECENT PHOTOGRAPH shows the statue of General Booth, which was unveiled by his
granddaughter, Commissioner Catherine Bramwell-Booth, at the opening of the complex. The
statue, in a typical stance, is a copy of the original at the Salvation Army's training college in
Denmark Hill, London. The birthplace, which like the rest of the terrace was built by William
Booth's father, contains a museum devoted to the Salvationist's life.

THE MIDLANDS
INDUSTRIAL EXHIBITION

THE MIDLANDS INDUSTRIAL Exhibition, Trent Bridge, in 1903 (left). The main building, in Indian style, was devoted to exhibits from around the world with Africans, Arabs, Indians and many other races showing their wares. There was also a funfair with a Canadian water chute, a Mexican toboggan and a fairy river. Other attractions included a maze, a biograph pavilion, concert hall, Japanese tea house and a high wire walker. Unfortunately, the fair remained for only a year before being burnt down in July 1904. On the left of the exhibition is A.J. Witty's boathouse and on the far left is the boathouse of the Nottingham Rowing Club. The club, which is the oldest in Nottingham as it was founded in 1862, later merged with the Nottingham Union Rowing Club.

IN THE RECENT photograph the boathouse on the left belongs to the Nottingham Boat Club. The building on the right was originally the Bridgford Hotel, constructed in 1964 and later became the offices of the Rushcliffe Borough Council.

NORTH WILFORD

NORTH WILFORD IN 1956 (left). On the left is the gatehouse of the Wilford Toll Bridge, known locally as the 'Ha'penny Bridge' from the toll made for pedestrians. The bridge was closed to cars in 1974 as it was unsafe and rebuilt in 1982 when it opened for pedestrians and cyclists only. In the distance are the chimneys of the North Wilford Power Station, and, on the right of the photograph, the Clifton Colliery, which supplied the coal for the power station generators. The colliery closed when it was no longer economic, and the power station followed in 1981.

THE WILFORD BRIDGE is no longer a toll bridge, but there is still a toll board indicating the charges once made for vehicles and animals. Sixpence was charged for every horse or beast drawing a carriage, fourpence for every horse drawing a cart and a penny for every ass carrying more than one person. The bridge has been widened and strengthened and now carries the new tramlines over the River Trent.

Other titles published by The History Press

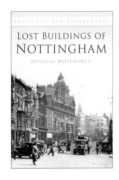

The Lost Buildings of Nottingham

DOUGLAS WHITWORTH

Nottingham, in common with many other English cities, experienced great changes during the twentieth century. This book illustrates the major buildings and many of the minor structures which were lost during that period. *The Lost Buildings of Nottingham* will also revive memories of much-loved buildings in the city, and provide a valuable record of what has been lost.

978 0 7524 5487 0

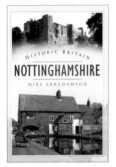

Historic Britain – Nottinghamshire

MIKE ABRAHAMSON

A fact-filled and entertaining guide to Nottinghamshire's most historic sites, which uncovers many lesser-known aspects of the county's past, such as the exciting story of how Eakring Oilwell played an important part in winning the Second World War. With full contact and access details, many archive images and stunning modern photographs, this intriguing guidebook will delight residents and visitors alike.

978 0 7524 5352 1

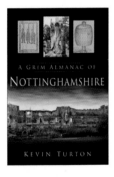

A Grim Almanac of Nottinghamshire

KEVIN TURTON

A collection of grim tales from the county, including that of the 'resurrection men' who, in 1826, stole thirty bodies from the graveyard of St Mary's church in Nottingham to sell to unscrupulous medical establishments in London. It emerged they had been shipping their cargo to the capital in wicker baskets booked aboard stagecoaches, but they were never caught. Not for the faint hearted!

978 0 7524 5593 8

Heroes & Villains of Nottingham

ADAM NIGHTINGALE

This fascinating collection of biographies chronicles the lives of some of Nottingham's most famous (and in some cases infamous) personalities. Including Civil War legends such as Colonel John Hutchinson, Naval adventurer Edward Fenton – who sailed with the pirate Martin Frobisher in search of the Northwest passage – and Victoria Cross winning air aces, as well as brave soldiers who fought against enemies such as the Zulus, the Spanish, the Confederates and the King.

978 0 7524 4924 1

Visit our website and discover thousands of other History Press books.

www.thehistorypress.co.uk